STUDENT DRIVER LOG BOOK

THIS LOG BOOK BELONGS TO

Name

Address

Phone

Email

DENBARNES PRESS

Date	

Time Started		Time Finished	

Weather Conditions	

Skills Practiced

Type of Driving (City, Highway, Rural...)

Day Minutes		Night Minutes		Total Minutes	
Carried Forward		Carried Forward		Carried Forward	
Total to Date		Total to Date		Total to Date	

Notes

Instructor	
Instructor's Signature	

Date	

Time Started		Time Finished	

Weather Conditions	

Skills Practiced

Type of Driving (City, Highway, Rural...)

Day Minutes		Night Minutes		Total Minutes	
Carried Forward		Carried Forward		Carried Forward	
Total to Date		Total to Date		Total to Date	

Notes

Instructor	
Instructor's Signature	

Date	

Time Started		Time Finished	

Weather Conditions	

Skills Practiced

Type of Driving (City, Highway, Rural...)

Day Minutes		Night Minutes		Total Minutes	
Carried Forward		Carried Forward		Carried Forward	
Total to Date		Total to Date		Total to Date	

Notes

Instructor	

Instructor's Signature	

Date	

Time Started		Time Finished	

Weather Conditions	

Skills Practiced

Type of Driving (City, Highway, Rural...)

Day Minutes		Night Minutes		Total Minutes	
Carried Forward		Carried Forward		Carried Forward	
Total to Date		Total to Date		Total to Date	

Notes

Instructor	

Instructor's Signature	

Date	

Time Started		Time Finished	

Weather Conditions	

Skills Practiced

Type of Driving (City, Highway, Rural...)

Day Minutes		Night Minutes		Total Minutes	
Carried Forward		Carried Forward		Carried Forward	
Total to Date		Total to Date		Total to Date	

Notes

Instructor	
Instructor's Signature	

Date	

Time Started		Time Finished	

Weather Conditions	

Skills Practiced

Type of Driving (City, Highway, Rural...)

Day Minutes		Night Minutes		Total Minutes	
Carried Forward		Carried Forward		Carried Forward	
Total to Date		Total to Date		Total to Date	

Notes

Instructor	
Instructor's Signature	

Date	

Time Started		Time Finished	

Weather Conditions	

Skills Practiced

Type of Driving (City, Highway, Rural...)

Day Minutes		Night Minutes		Total Minutes	
Carried Forward		Carried Forward		Carried Forward	
Total to Date		Total to Date		Total to Date	

Notes

Instructor	

Instructor's Signature	

Date	

Time Started		Time Finished	

Weather Conditions	

Skills Practiced

Type of Driving (City, Highway, Rural...)

Day Minutes		Night Minutes		Total Minutes	
Carried Forward		Carried Forward		Carried Forward	
Total to Date		Total to Date		Total to Date	

Notes

Instructor	

Instructor's Signature	

Date	

Time Started		Time Finished	

Weather Conditions	

Skills Practiced

Type of Driving (City, Highway, Rural...)

Day Minutes		Night Minutes		Total Minutes	
Carried Forward		Carried Forward		Carried Forward	
Total to Date		Total to Date		Total to Date	

Notes

Instructor	
Instructor's Signature	

Date	

Time Started		Time Finished	

Weather Conditions	

Skills Practiced

Type of Driving (City, Highway, Rural...)

Day Minutes		Night Minutes		Total Minutes	
Carried Forward		Carried Forward		Carried Forward	
Total to Date		Total to Date		Total to Date	

Notes

Instructor	
Instructor's Signature	

Date	

Time Started		Time Finished	

Weather Conditions	

Skills Practiced

Type of Driving (City, Highway, Rural...)

Day Minutes		Night Minutes		Total Minutes	
Carried Forward		Carried Forward		Carried Forward	
Total to Date		Total to Date		Total to Date	

Notes

Instructor	
Instructor's Signature	

Date	

Time Started		Time Finished	

Weather Conditions	

Skills Practiced

Type of Driving (City, Highway, Rural...)

Day Minutes		Night Minutes		Total Minutes	
Carried Forward		Carried Forward		Carried Forward	
Total to Date		Total to Date		Total to Date	

Notes

Instructor	
Instructor's Signature	

Date	

Time Started		Time Finished	

Weather Conditions	

Skills Practiced

Type of Driving (City, Highway, Rural...)

Day Minutes		Night Minutes		Total Minutes	
Carried Forward		Carried Forward		Carried Forward	
Total to Date		Total to Date		Total to Date	

Notes

Instructor	

Instructor's Signature	

Date	

Time Started		Time Finished	

Weather Conditions	

Skills Practiced

Type of Driving (City, Highway, Rural...)

Day Minutes		Night Minutes		Total Minutes	
Carried Forward		Carried Forward		Carried Forward	
Total to Date		Total to Date		Total to Date	

Notes

Instructor	

Instructor's Signature	

Date	

Time Started		Time Finished	

Weather Conditions	

Skills Practiced

Type of Driving (City, Highway, Rural...)

Day Minutes		Night Minutes		Total Minutes	
Carried Forward		Carried Forward		Carried Forward	
Total to Date		Total to Date		Total to Date	

Notes

Instructor	

Instructor's Signature	

Date	

Time Started		Time Finished	

Weather Conditions	

Skills Practiced

Type of Driving (City, Highway, Rural...)

Day Minutes		Night Minutes		Total Minutes	
Carried Forward		Carried Forward		Carried Forward	
Total to Date		Total to Date		Total to Date	

Notes

Instructor	

Instructor's Signature	

Date	

Time Started		Time Finished	

Weather Conditions	

Skills Practiced

Type of Driving (City, Highway, Rural...)

Day Minutes		Night Minutes		Total Minutes	
Carried Forward		Carried Forward		Carried Forward	
Total to Date		Total to Date		Total to Date	

Notes

Instructor	

Instructor's Signature	

Date	

Time Started		Time Finished	

Weather Conditions	

Skills Practiced

Type of Driving (City, Highway, Rural...)

Day Minutes		Night Minutes		Total Minutes	
Carried Forward		Carried Forward		Carried Forward	
Total to Date		Total to Date		Total to Date	

Notes

Instructor	

Instructor's Signature	

Date	

Time Started		Time Finished	

Weather Conditions	

Skills Practiced

Type of Driving (City, Highway, Rural...)

Day Minutes		Night Minutes		Total Minutes	
Carried Forward		Carried Forward		Carried Forward	
Total to Date		Total to Date		Total to Date	

Notes

Instructor	

Instructor's Signature	

Date	

Time Started		Time Finished	

Weather Conditions	

Skills Practiced

Type of Driving (City, Highway, Rural...)

Day Minutes		Night Minutes		Total Minutes	
Carried Forward		Carried Forward		Carried Forward	
Total to Date		Total to Date		Total to Date	

Notes

Instructor	

Instructor's Signature	

Date	

Time Started		Time Finished	

Weather Conditions	

Skills Practiced

Type of Driving (City, Highway, Rural...)

Day Minutes		Night Minutes		Total Minutes	
Carried Forward		Carried Forward		Carried Forward	
Total to Date		Total to Date		Total to Date	

Notes

Instructor	

Instructor's Signature	

Date	

Time Started		Time Finished	

Weather Conditions	

Skills Practiced

Type of Driving (City, Highway, Rural...)

Day Minutes		Night Minutes		Total Minutes	
Carried Forward		Carried Forward		Carried Forward	
Total to Date		Total to Date		Total to Date	

Notes

Instructor	

Instructor's Signature	

Date	

Time Started		Time Finished	

Weather Conditions	

Skills Practiced

Type of Driving (City, Highway, Rural...)

Day Minutes		Night Minutes		Total Minutes	
Carried Forward		Carried Forward		Carried Forward	
Total to Date		Total to Date		Total to Date	

Notes

Instructor	
Instructor's Signature	

Date	

Time Started		Time Finished	

Weather Conditions	

Skills Practiced

Type of Driving (City, Highway, Rural...)

Day Minutes		Night Minutes		Total Minutes	
Carried Forward		Carried Forward		Carried Forward	
Total to Date		Total to Date		Total to Date	

Notes

Instructor	
Instructor's Signature	

Date	

Time Started		Time Finished	

Weather Conditions	

Skills Practiced

Type of Driving (City, Highway, Rural...)

Day Minutes		Night Minutes		Total Minutes	
Carried Forward		Carried Forward		Carried Forward	
Total to Date		Total to Date		Total to Date	

Notes

Instructor	

Instructor's Signature	

Date	

Time Started		Time Finished	

Weather Conditions	

Skills Practiced

Type of Driving (City, Highway, Rural...)

Day Minutes		Night Minutes		Total Minutes	
Carried Forward		Carried Forward		Carried Forward	
Total to Date		Total to Date		Total to Date	

Notes

Instructor	

Instructor's Signature	

Date	

Time Started		Time Finished	

Weather Conditions	

Skills Practiced

Type of Driving (City, Highway, Rural...)

Day Minutes		Night Minutes		Total Minutes	
Carried Forward		Carried Forward		Carried Forward	
Total to Date		Total to Date		Total to Date	

Notes	

Instructor	
Instructor's Signature	

Date	

Time Started		Time Finished	

Weather Conditions	

Skills Practiced

Type of Driving (City, Highway, Rural...)

Day Minutes		Night Minutes		Total Minutes	
Carried Forward		Carried Forward		Carried Forward	
Total to Date		Total to Date		Total to Date	

Notes	

Instructor	
Instructor's Signature	

Date	
Time Started		Time Finished	
Weather Conditions	
Skills Practiced	
Type of Driving (City, Highway, Rural...)	

Day Minutes		Night Minutes		Total Minutes	
Carried Forward		Carried Forward		Carried Forward	
Total to Date		Total to Date		Total to Date	

Notes	
Instructor	
Instructor's Signature	

Date	
Time Started		Time Finished	
Weather Conditions	
Skills Practiced	
Type of Driving (City, Highway, Rural...)	

Day Minutes		Night Minutes		Total Minutes	
Carried Forward		Carried Forward		Carried Forward	
Total to Date		Total to Date		Total to Date	

Notes	
Instructor	
Instructor's Signature	

Date	

Time Started		Time Finished	

Weather Conditions	

Skills Practiced

Type of Driving (City, Highway, Rural...)

Day Minutes		Night Minutes		Total Minutes	
Carried Forward		Carried Forward		Carried Forward	
Total to Date		Total to Date		Total to Date	

Notes

Instructor	

Instructor's Signature	

Date	

Time Started		Time Finished	

Weather Conditions	

Skills Practiced

Type of Driving (City, Highway, Rural...)

Day Minutes		Night Minutes		Total Minutes	
Carried Forward		Carried Forward		Carried Forward	
Total to Date		Total to Date		Total to Date	

Notes

Instructor	

Instructor's Signature	

Date	

Time Started		Time Finished	

Weather Conditions	

Skills Practiced

Type of Driving (City, Highway, Rural...)

Day Minutes		Night Minutes		Total Minutes	
Carried Forward		Carried Forward		Carried Forward	
Total to Date		Total to Date		Total to Date	

Notes

Instructor	
Instructor's Signature	

Date	

Time Started		Time Finished	

Weather Conditions	

Skills Practiced

Type of Driving (City, Highway, Rural...)

Day Minutes		Night Minutes		Total Minutes	
Carried Forward		Carried Forward		Carried Forward	
Total to Date		Total to Date		Total to Date	

Notes

Instructor	
Instructor's Signature	

Date	

Time Started		Time Finished	

Weather Conditions	

Skills Practiced

Type of Driving (City, Highway, Rural...)

Day Minutes		Night Minutes		Total Minutes	
Carried Forward		Carried Forward		Carried Forward	
Total to Date		Total to Date		Total to Date	

Notes

Instructor	

Instructor's Signature	

Date	

Time Started		Time Finished	

Weather Conditions	

Skills Practiced

Type of Driving (City, Highway, Rural...)

Day Minutes		Night Minutes		Total Minutes	
Carried Forward		Carried Forward		Carried Forward	
Total to Date		Total to Date		Total to Date	

Notes

Instructor	

Instructor's Signature	

Date	

Time Started		Time Finished	

Weather Conditions	

Skills Practiced

Type of Driving (City, Highway, Rural...)

Day Minutes		Night Minutes		Total Minutes	
Carried Forward		Carried Forward		Carried Forward	
Total to Date		Total to Date		Total to Date	

Notes

Instructor	
Instructor's Signature	

Date	

Time Started		Time Finished	

Weather Conditions	

Skills Practiced

Type of Driving (City, Highway, Rural...)

Day Minutes		Night Minutes		Total Minutes	
Carried Forward		Carried Forward		Carried Forward	
Total to Date		Total to Date		Total to Date	

Notes

Instructor	
Instructor's Signature	

Date	

Time Started		Time Finished	

Weather Conditions	

Skills Practiced

Type of Driving (City, Highway, Rural...)

Day Minutes		Night Minutes		Total Minutes	
Carried Forward		Carried Forward		Carried Forward	
Total to Date		Total to Date		Total to Date	

Notes

Instructor	
Instructor's Signature	

Date	

Time Started		Time Finished	

Weather Conditions	

Skills Practiced

Type of Driving (City, Highway, Rural...)

Day Minutes		Night Minutes		Total Minutes	
Carried Forward		Carried Forward		Carried Forward	
Total to Date		Total to Date		Total to Date	

Notes

Instructor	
Instructor's Signature	

Date	

Time Started		Time Finished	

Weather Conditions	

Skills Practiced

Type of Driving (City, Highway, Rural...)

Day Minutes		Night Minutes		Total Minutes	
Carried Forward		Carried Forward		Carried Forward	
Total to Date		Total to Date		Total to Date	

Notes

Instructor	

Instructor's Signature	

Date	

Time Started		Time Finished	

Weather Conditions	

Skills Practiced

Type of Driving (City, Highway, Rural...)

Day Minutes		Night Minutes		Total Minutes	
Carried Forward		Carried Forward		Carried Forward	
Total to Date		Total to Date		Total to Date	

Notes

Instructor	

Instructor's Signature	

Date	
Time Started		Time Finished	
Weather Conditions	
Skills Practiced	
Type of Driving (City, Highway, Rural...)	

Day Minutes		Night Minutes		Total Minutes	
Carried Forward		Carried Forward		Carried Forward	
Total to Date		Total to Date		Total to Date	

Notes	
Instructor	
Instructor's Signature	

Date	
Time Started		Time Finished	
Weather Conditions	
Skills Practiced	
Type of Driving (City, Highway, Rural...)	

Day Minutes		Night Minutes		Total Minutes	
Carried Forward		Carried Forward		Carried Forward	
Total to Date		Total to Date		Total to Date	

Notes	
Instructor	
Instructor's Signature	

Date	

Time Started		Time Finished	

Weather Conditions	

Skills Practiced

Type of Driving (City, Highway, Rural...)

Day Minutes		Night Minutes		Total Minutes	
Carried Forward		Carried Forward		Carried Forward	
Total to Date		Total to Date		Total to Date	

Notes

Instructor	

Instructor's Signature	

Date	

Time Started		Time Finished	

Weather Conditions	

Skills Practiced

Type of Driving (City, Highway, Rural...)

Day Minutes		Night Minutes		Total Minutes	
Carried Forward		Carried Forward		Carried Forward	
Total to Date		Total to Date		Total to Date	

Notes

Instructor	

Instructor's Signature	

Date	

Time Started		Time Finished	

Weather Conditions	

Skills Practiced

Type of Driving (City, Highway, Rural...)

Day Minutes		Night Minutes		Total Minutes	
Carried Forward		Carried Forward		Carried Forward	
Total to Date		Total to Date		Total to Date	

Notes

Instructor	

Instructor's Signature	

Date	

Time Started		Time Finished	

Weather Conditions	

Skills Practiced

Type of Driving (City, Highway, Rural...)

Day Minutes		Night Minutes		Total Minutes	
Carried Forward		Carried Forward		Carried Forward	
Total to Date		Total to Date		Total to Date	

Notes

Instructor	

Instructor's Signature	

Date	

Time Started		Time Finished	

Weather Conditions	

Skills Practiced

Type of Driving (City, Highway, Rural...)

Day Minutes		Night Minutes		Total Minutes	
Carried Forward		Carried Forward		Carried Forward	
Total to Date		Total to Date		Total to Date	

Notes

Instructor	

Instructor's Signature	

Date	

Time Started		Time Finished	

Weather Conditions	

Skills Practiced

Type of Driving (City, Highway, Rural...)

Day Minutes		Night Minutes		Total Minutes	
Carried Forward		Carried Forward		Carried Forward	
Total to Date		Total to Date		Total to Date	

Notes

Instructor	

Instructor's Signature	

Date	
Time Started		Time Finished	
Weather Conditions	
Skills Practiced	
Type of Driving (City, Highway, Rural...)	

Day Minutes		Night Minutes		Total Minutes	
Carried Forward		Carried Forward		Carried Forward	
Total to Date		Total to Date		Total to Date	

Notes	
Instructor	
Instructor's Signature	

Date	
Time Started		Time Finished	
Weather Conditions	
Skills Practiced	
Type of Driving (City, Highway, Rural...)	

Day Minutes		Night Minutes		Total Minutes	
Carried Forward		Carried Forward		Carried Forward	
Total to Date		Total to Date		Total to Date	

Notes	
Instructor	
Instructor's Signature	

Date	

Time Started		Time Finished	

Weather Conditions	

Skills Practiced

Type of Driving (City, Highway, Rural...)

Day Minutes		Night Minutes		Total Minutes	
Carried Forward		Carried Forward		Carried Forward	
Total to Date		Total to Date		Total to Date	

Notes

Instructor	
Instructor's Signature	

Date	

Time Started		Time Finished	

Weather Conditions	

Skills Practiced

Type of Driving (City, Highway, Rural...)

Day Minutes		Night Minutes		Total Minutes	
Carried Forward		Carried Forward		Carried Forward	
Total to Date		Total to Date		Total to Date	

Notes

Instructor	
Instructor's Signature	

Date	

Time Started		Time Finished	

Weather Conditions	

Skills Practiced

Type of Driving (City, Highway, Rural...)

Day Minutes		Night Minutes		Total Minutes	
Carried Forward		Carried Forward		Carried Forward	
Total to Date		Total to Date		Total to Date	

Notes

Instructor	

Instructor's Signature	

Date	

Time Started		Time Finished	

Weather Conditions	

Skills Practiced

Type of Driving (City, Highway, Rural...)

Day Minutes		Night Minutes		Total Minutes	
Carried Forward		Carried Forward		Carried Forward	
Total to Date		Total to Date		Total to Date	

Notes

Instructor	

Instructor's Signature	

Date	
Time Started		**Time Finished**	
Weather Conditions	
Skills Practiced	

Type of Driving (City, Highway, Rural...)

Day Minutes		Night Minutes		Total Minutes	
Carried Forward		Carried Forward		Carried Forward	
Total to Date		Total to Date		Total to Date	

Notes	
Instructor	
Instructor's Signature	

Date	
Time Started		**Time Finished**	
Weather Conditions	
Skills Practiced	

Type of Driving (City, Highway, Rural...)

Day Minutes		Night Minutes		Total Minutes	
Carried Forward		Carried Forward		Carried Forward	
Total to Date		Total to Date		Total to Date	

Notes	
Instructor	
Instructor's Signature	

Date	

Time Started		Time Finished	

Weather Conditions	

Skills Practiced

Type of Driving (City, Highway, Rural...)

Day Minutes		Night Minutes		Total Minutes	
Carried Forward		Carried Forward		Carried Forward	
Total to Date		Total to Date		Total to Date	

Notes

Instructor	

Instructor's Signature	

Date	

Time Started		Time Finished	

Weather Conditions	

Skills Practiced

Type of Driving (City, Highway, Rural...)

Day Minutes		Night Minutes		Total Minutes	
Carried Forward		Carried Forward		Carried Forward	
Total to Date		Total to Date		Total to Date	

Notes

Instructor	

Instructor's Signature	

Date	

Time Started		Time Finished	

Weather Conditions	

Skills Practiced

Type of Driving (City, Highway, Rural...)

Day Minutes		Night Minutes		Total Minutes	
Carried Forward		Carried Forward		Carried Forward	
Total to Date		Total to Date		Total to Date	

Notes

Instructor	

Instructor's Signature	

Date	

Time Started		Time Finished	

Weather Conditions	

Skills Practiced

Type of Driving (City, Highway, Rural...)

Day Minutes		Night Minutes		Total Minutes	
Carried Forward		Carried Forward		Carried Forward	
Total to Date		Total to Date		Total to Date	

Notes

Instructor	

Instructor's Signature	

Date	

Time Started		Time Finished	

Weather Conditions	

Skills Practiced

Type of Driving (City, Highway, Rural...)

Day Minutes		Night Minutes		Total Minutes	
Carried Forward		Carried Forward		Carried Forward	
Total to Date		Total to Date		Total to Date	

Notes

Instructor	

Instructor's Signature	

Date	

Time Started		Time Finished	

Weather Conditions	

Skills Practiced

Type of Driving (City, Highway, Rural...)

Day Minutes		Night Minutes		Total Minutes	
Carried Forward		Carried Forward		Carried Forward	
Total to Date		Total to Date		Total to Date	

Notes

Instructor	

Instructor's Signature	

Date	

Time Started		Time Finished	

Weather Conditions	

Skills Practiced

Type of Driving (City, Highway, Rural...)

Day Minutes		Night Minutes		Total Minutes	
Carried Forward		Carried Forward		Carried Forward	
Total to Date		Total to Date		Total to Date	

Notes

Instructor	
Instructor's Signature	

Date	

Time Started		Time Finished	

Weather Conditions	

Skills Practiced

Type of Driving (City, Highway, Rural...)

Day Minutes		Night Minutes		Total Minutes	
Carried Forward		Carried Forward		Carried Forward	
Total to Date		Total to Date		Total to Date	

Notes

Instructor	
Instructor's Signature	

Date	
Time Started		**Time Finished**	

Weather Conditions	

Skills Practiced

Type of Driving (City, Highway, Rural...)

Day Minutes		Night Minutes		Total Minutes	
Carried Forward		Carried Forward		Carried Forward	
Total to Date		Total to Date		Total to Date	

Notes

Instructor	
Instructor's Signature	

Date	
Time Started		**Time Finished**	

Weather Conditions	

Skills Practiced

Type of Driving (City, Highway, Rural...)

Day Minutes		Night Minutes		Total Minutes	
Carried Forward		Carried Forward		Carried Forward	
Total to Date		Total to Date		Total to Date	

Notes

Instructor	
Instructor's Signature	

Date	

Time Started		Time Finished	

Weather Conditions	

Skills Practiced

Type of Driving (City, Highway, Rural...)

Day Minutes		Night Minutes		Total Minutes	
Carried Forward		Carried Forward		Carried Forward	
Total to Date		Total to Date		Total to Date	

Notes

Instructor	
Instructor's Signature	

Date	

Time Started		Time Finished	

Weather Conditions	

Skills Practiced

Type of Driving (City, Highway, Rural...)

Day Minutes		Night Minutes		Total Minutes	
Carried Forward		Carried Forward		Carried Forward	
Total to Date		Total to Date		Total to Date	

Notes

Instructor	
Instructor's Signature	

Date	

Time Started		Time Finished	

Weather Conditions	

Skills Practiced

Type of Driving (City, Highway, Rural...)

Day Minutes		Night Minutes		Total Minutes	
Carried Forward		Carried Forward		Carried Forward	
Total to Date		Total to Date		Total to Date	

Notes

Instructor	
Instructor's Signature	

Date	

Time Started		Time Finished	

Weather Conditions	

Skills Practiced

Type of Driving (City, Highway, Rural...)

Day Minutes		Night Minutes		Total Minutes	
Carried Forward		Carried Forward		Carried Forward	
Total to Date		Total to Date		Total to Date	

Notes

Instructor	
Instructor's Signature	

Date	

Time Started		Time Finished	

Weather Conditions	

Skills Practiced

Type of Driving (City, Highway, Rural...)

Day Minutes		Night Minutes		Total Minutes	
Carried Forward		Carried Forward		Carried Forward	
Total to Date		Total to Date		Total to Date	

Notes

Instructor	

Instructor's Signature	

Date	

Time Started		Time Finished	

Weather Conditions	

Skills Practiced

Type of Driving (City, Highway, Rural...)

Day Minutes		Night Minutes		Total Minutes	
Carried Forward		Carried Forward		Carried Forward	
Total to Date		Total to Date		Total to Date	

Notes

Instructor	

Instructor's Signature	

Date	

Time Started		Time Finished	

Weather Conditions	

Skills Practiced

Type of Driving (City, Highway, Rural...)

Day Minutes		Night Minutes		Total Minutes	
Carried Forward		Carried Forward		Carried Forward	
Total to Date		Total to Date		Total to Date	

Notes

Instructor	

Instructor's Signature	

Date	

Time Started		Time Finished	

Weather Conditions	

Skills Practiced

Type of Driving (City, Highway, Rural...)

Day Minutes		Night Minutes		Total Minutes	
Carried Forward		Carried Forward		Carried Forward	
Total to Date		Total to Date		Total to Date	

Notes

Instructor	

Instructor's Signature	

Date	
Time Started		Time Finished	
Weather Conditions	
Skills Practiced	
Type of Driving (City, Highway, Rural…)	

Day Minutes		Night Minutes		Total Minutes	
Carried Forward		Carried Forward		Carried Forward	
Total to Date		Total to Date		Total to Date	

Notes	
Instructor	
Instructor's Signature	

Date	
Time Started		Time Finished	
Weather Conditions	
Skills Practiced	
Type of Driving (City, Highway, Rural…)	

Day Minutes		Night Minutes		Total Minutes	
Carried Forward		Carried Forward		Carried Forward	
Total to Date		Total to Date		Total to Date	

Notes	
Instructor	
Instructor's Signature	

Date	
Time Started		Time Finished	
Weather Conditions	
Skills Practiced	
Type of Driving (City, Highway, Rural...)	

Day Minutes		Night Minutes		Total Minutes	
Carried Forward		Carried Forward		Carried Forward	
Total to Date		Total to Date		Total to Date	

Notes	
Instructor	
Instructor's Signature	

Date	
Time Started		Time Finished	
Weather Conditions	
Skills Practiced	
Type of Driving (City, Highway, Rural...)	

Day Minutes		Night Minutes		Total Minutes	
Carried Forward		Carried Forward		Carried Forward	
Total to Date		Total to Date		Total to Date	

Notes	
Instructor	
Instructor's Signature	

Date	

Time Started		Time Finished	

Weather Conditions	

Skills Practiced

Type of Driving (City, Highway, Rural…)

Day Minutes		Night Minutes		Total Minutes	
Carried Forward		Carried Forward		Carried Forward	
Total to Date		Total to Date		Total to Date	

Notes

Instructor	
Instructor's Signature	

Date	

Time Started		Time Finished	

Weather Conditions	

Skills Practiced

Type of Driving (City, Highway, Rural…)

Day Minutes		Night Minutes		Total Minutes	
Carried Forward		Carried Forward		Carried Forward	
Total to Date		Total to Date		Total to Date	

Notes

Instructor	
Instructor's Signature	

Date	

Time Started		Time Finished	

Weather Conditions	

Skills Practiced

Type of Driving (City, Highway, Rural...)

Day Minutes		Night Minutes		Total Minutes	
Carried Forward		Carried Forward		Carried Forward	
Total to Date		Total to Date		Total to Date	

Notes

Instructor	
Instructor's Signature	

Date	

Time Started		Time Finished	

Weather Conditions	

Skills Practiced

Type of Driving (City, Highway, Rural...)

Day Minutes		Night Minutes		Total Minutes	
Carried Forward		Carried Forward		Carried Forward	
Total to Date		Total to Date		Total to Date	

Notes

Instructor	
Instructor's Signature	

Date	

Time Started		Time Finished	

Weather Conditions	

Skills Practiced

Type of Driving (City, Highway, Rural...)

Day Minutes		Night Minutes		Total Minutes	
Carried Forward		Carried Forward		Carried Forward	
Total to Date		Total to Date		Total to Date	

Notes

Instructor	

Instructor's Signature	

Date	

Time Started		Time Finished	

Weather Conditions	

Skills Practiced

Type of Driving (City, Highway, Rural...)

Day Minutes		Night Minutes		Total Minutes	
Carried Forward		Carried Forward		Carried Forward	
Total to Date		Total to Date		Total to Date	

Notes

Instructor	

Instructor's Signature	

Date	
Time Started		Time Finished	
Weather Conditions	
Skills Practiced	
Type of Driving (City, Highway, Rural...)	

Day Minutes		Night Minutes		Total Minutes	
Carried Forward		Carried Forward		Carried Forward	
Total to Date		Total to Date		Total to Date	

Notes	
Instructor	
Instructor's Signature	

Date	
Time Started		Time Finished	
Weather Conditions	
Skills Practiced	
Type of Driving (City, Highway, Rural...)	

Day Minutes		Night Minutes		Total Minutes	
Carried Forward		Carried Forward		Carried Forward	
Total to Date		Total to Date		Total to Date	

Notes	
Instructor	
Instructor's Signature	

Date	

Time Started		Time Finished	

Weather Conditions	

Skills Practiced

Type of Driving (City, Highway, Rural...)

Day Minutes		Night Minutes		Total Minutes	
Carried Forward		Carried Forward		Carried Forward	
Total to Date		Total to Date		Total to Date	

Notes

Instructor	
Instructor's Signature	

Date	

Time Started		Time Finished	

Weather Conditions	

Skills Practiced

Type of Driving (City, Highway, Rural...)

Day Minutes		Night Minutes		Total Minutes	
Carried Forward		Carried Forward		Carried Forward	
Total to Date		Total to Date		Total to Date	

Notes

Instructor	
Instructor's Signature	

Date	

Time Started		Time Finished	

Weather Conditions	

Skills Practiced

Type of Driving (City, Highway, Rural...)

Day Minutes		Night Minutes		Total Minutes	
Carried Forward		Carried Forward		Carried Forward	
Total to Date		Total to Date		Total to Date	

Notes

Instructor	

Instructor's Signature	

Date	

Time Started		Time Finished	

Weather Conditions	

Skills Practiced

Type of Driving (City, Highway, Rural...)

Day Minutes		Night Minutes		Total Minutes	
Carried Forward		Carried Forward		Carried Forward	
Total to Date		Total to Date		Total to Date	

Notes

Instructor	

Instructor's Signature	

Date	

Time Started		Time Finished	

Weather Conditions	

Skills Practiced

Type of Driving (City, Highway, Rural...)

Day Minutes		Night Minutes		Total Minutes	
Carried Forward		Carried Forward		Carried Forward	
Total to Date		Total to Date		Total to Date	

Notes

Instructor	
Instructor's Signature	

Date	

Time Started		Time Finished	

Weather Conditions	

Skills Practiced

Type of Driving (City, Highway, Rural...)

Day Minutes		Night Minutes		Total Minutes	
Carried Forward		Carried Forward		Carried Forward	
Total to Date		Total to Date		Total to Date	

Notes

Instructor	
Instructor's Signature	

Date	

Time Started		Time Finished	

Weather Conditions	

Skills Practiced	

Type of Driving (City, Highway, Rural...)	

Day Minutes		Night Minutes		Total Minutes	
Carried Forward		Carried Forward		Carried Forward	
Total to Date		Total to Date		Total to Date	

Notes	

Instructor	

Instructor's Signature	

Date	

Time Started		Time Finished	

Weather Conditions	

Skills Practiced	

Type of Driving (City, Highway, Rural...)	

Day Minutes		Night Minutes		Total Minutes	
Carried Forward		Carried Forward		Carried Forward	
Total to Date		Total to Date		Total to Date	

Notes	

Instructor	

Instructor's Signature	

Date	

Time Started		Time Finished	

Weather Conditions	

Skills Practiced

Type of Driving (City, Highway, Rural...)

Day Minutes		Night Minutes		Total Minutes	
Carried Forward		Carried Forward		Carried Forward	
Total to Date		Total to Date		Total to Date	

Notes

Instructor	
Instructor's Signature	

Date	

Time Started		Time Finished	

Weather Conditions	

Skills Practiced

Type of Driving (City, Highway, Rural...)

Day Minutes		Night Minutes		Total Minutes	
Carried Forward		Carried Forward		Carried Forward	
Total to Date		Total to Date		Total to Date	

Notes

Instructor	
Instructor's Signature	

Date	

Time Started		Time Finished	

Weather Conditions	

Skills Practiced

Type of Driving (City, Highway, Rural...)

Day Minutes		Night Minutes		Total Minutes	
Carried Forward		Carried Forward		Carried Forward	
Total to Date		Total to Date		Total to Date	

Notes

Instructor	
Instructor's Signature	

Date	

Time Started		Time Finished	

Weather Conditions	

Skills Practiced

Type of Driving (City, Highway, Rural...)

Day Minutes		Night Minutes		Total Minutes	
Carried Forward		Carried Forward		Carried Forward	
Total to Date		Total to Date		Total to Date	

Notes

Instructor	
Instructor's Signature	

Date	
Time Started		Time Finished	
Weather Conditions	
Skills Practiced	
Type of Driving (City, Highway, Rural...)	

Day Minutes		Night Minutes		Total Minutes	
Carried Forward		Carried Forward		Carried Forward	
Total to Date		Total to Date		Total to Date	

Notes	
Instructor	
Instructor's Signature	

Date	
Time Started		Time Finished	
Weather Conditions	
Skills Practiced	
Type of Driving (City, Highway, Rural...)	

Day Minutes		Night Minutes		Total Minutes	
Carried Forward		Carried Forward		Carried Forward	
Total to Date		Total to Date		Total to Date	

Notes	
Instructor	
Instructor's Signature	

Date	

Time Started		Time Finished	

Weather Conditions	

Skills Practiced

Type of Driving (City, Highway, Rural...)

Day Minutes		Night Minutes		Total Minutes	
Carried Forward		Carried Forward		Carried Forward	
Total to Date		Total to Date		Total to Date	

Notes

Instructor	

Instructor's Signature	

Date	

Time Started		Time Finished	

Weather Conditions	

Skills Practiced

Type of Driving (City, Highway, Rural...)

Day Minutes		Night Minutes		Total Minutes	
Carried Forward		Carried Forward		Carried Forward	
Total to Date		Total to Date		Total to Date	

Notes

Instructor	

Instructor's Signature	

Date	

Time Started		Time Finished	

Weather Conditions	

Skills Practiced

Type of Driving (City, Highway, Rural...)

Day Minutes		Night Minutes		Total Minutes	
Carried Forward		Carried Forward		Carried Forward	
Total to Date		Total to Date		Total to Date	

Notes

Instructor	

Instructor's Signature	

Date	

Time Started		Time Finished	

Weather Conditions	

Skills Practiced

Type of Driving (City, Highway, Rural...)

Day Minutes		Night Minutes		Total Minutes	
Carried Forward		Carried Forward		Carried Forward	
Total to Date		Total to Date		Total to Date	

Notes

Instructor	

Instructor's Signature	

Date	
Time Started		Time Finished	
Weather Conditions	
Skills Practiced	
Type of Driving (City, Highway, Rural...)	

Day Minutes		Night Minutes		Total Minutes	
Carried Forward		Carried Forward		Carried Forward	
Total to Date		Total to Date		Total to Date	

Notes	
Instructor	
Instructor's Signature	

Date	
Time Started		Time Finished	
Weather Conditions	
Skills Practiced	
Type of Driving (City, Highway, Rural...)	

Day Minutes		Night Minutes		Total Minutes	
Carried Forward		Carried Forward		Carried Forward	
Total to Date		Total to Date		Total to Date	

Notes	
Instructor	
Instructor's Signature	

Date	

Time Started		Time Finished	

Weather Conditions	

Skills Practiced

Type of Driving (City, Highway, Rural...)

Day Minutes		Night Minutes		Total Minutes	
Carried Forward		Carried Forward		Carried Forward	
Total to Date		Total to Date		Total to Date	

Notes

Instructor	

Instructor's Signature	

Date	

Time Started		Time Finished	

Weather Conditions	

Skills Practiced

Type of Driving (City, Highway, Rural...)

Day Minutes		Night Minutes		Total Minutes	
Carried Forward		Carried Forward		Carried Forward	
Total to Date		Total to Date		Total to Date	

Notes

Instructor	

Instructor's Signature	

Date	

Time Started		Time Finished	

Weather Conditions	

Skills Practiced

Type of Driving (City, Highway, Rural...)

Day Minutes		Night Minutes		Total Minutes	
Carried Forward		Carried Forward		Carried Forward	
Total to Date		Total to Date		Total to Date	

Notes	

Instructor	
Instructor's Signature	

Date	

Time Started		Time Finished	

Weather Conditions	

Skills Practiced

Type of Driving (City, Highway, Rural...)

Day Minutes		Night Minutes		Total Minutes	
Carried Forward		Carried Forward		Carried Forward	
Total to Date		Total to Date		Total to Date	

Notes	

Instructor	
Instructor's Signature	

Date	

Time Started		Time Finished	

Weather Conditions	

Skills Practiced

Type of Driving (City, Highway, Rural...)

Day Minutes		Night Minutes		Total Minutes	
Carried Forward		Carried Forward		Carried Forward	
Total to Date		Total to Date		Total to Date	

Notes

Instructor	
Instructor's Signature	

Date	

Time Started		Time Finished	

Weather Conditions	

Skills Practiced

Type of Driving (City, Highway, Rural...)

Day Minutes		Night Minutes		Total Minutes	
Carried Forward		Carried Forward		Carried Forward	
Total to Date		Total to Date		Total to Date	

Notes

Instructor	
Instructor's Signature	

Date	

Time Started		Time Finished	

Weather Conditions	

Skills Practiced

Type of Driving (City, Highway, Rural...)

Day Minutes		Night Minutes		Total Minutes	
Carried Forward		Carried Forward		Carried Forward	
Total to Date		Total to Date		Total to Date	

Notes

Instructor	
Instructor's Signature	

Date	

Time Started		Time Finished	

Weather Conditions	

Skills Practiced

Type of Driving (City, Highway, Rural...)

Day Minutes		Night Minutes		Total Minutes	
Carried Forward		Carried Forward		Carried Forward	
Total to Date		Total to Date		Total to Date	

Notes

Instructor	
Instructor's Signature	

Date	
Time Started		**Time Finished**	
Weather Conditions	
Skills Practiced	

Type of Driving (City, Highway, Rural...)

Day Minutes		Night Minutes		Total Minutes	
Carried Forward		Carried Forward		Carried Forward	
Total to Date		Total to Date		Total to Date	

Notes

Instructor	
Instructor's Signature	

Date	
Time Started		**Time Finished**	
Weather Conditions	
Skills Practiced	

Type of Driving (City, Highway, Rural...)

Day Minutes		Night Minutes		Total Minutes	
Carried Forward		Carried Forward		Carried Forward	
Total to Date		Total to Date		Total to Date	

Notes

Instructor	
Instructor's Signature	

Date	

Time Started		Time Finished	

Weather Conditions	

Skills Practiced

Type of Driving (City, Highway, Rural...)

Day Minutes		Night Minutes		Total Minutes	
Carried Forward		Carried Forward		Carried Forward	
Total to Date		Total to Date		Total to Date	

Notes

Instructor	
Instructor's Signature	

Date	

Time Started		Time Finished	

Weather Conditions	

Skills Practiced

Type of Driving (City, Highway, Rural...)

Day Minutes		Night Minutes		Total Minutes	
Carried Forward		Carried Forward		Carried Forward	
Total to Date		Total to Date		Total to Date	

Notes

Instructor	
Instructor's Signature	

Date	

Time Started		Time Finished	

Weather Conditions	

Skills Practiced

Type of Driving (City, Highway, Rural...)

Day Minutes		Night Minutes		Total Minutes	
Carried Forward		Carried Forward		Carried Forward	
Total to Date		Total to Date		Total to Date	

Notes

Instructor	
Instructor's Signature	

Date	

Time Started		Time Finished	

Weather Conditions	

Skills Practiced

Type of Driving (City, Highway, Rural...)

Day Minutes		Night Minutes		Total Minutes	
Carried Forward		Carried Forward		Carried Forward	
Total to Date		Total to Date		Total to Date	

Notes

Instructor	
Instructor's Signature	

Date	

Time Started		Time Finished	

Weather Conditions	

Skills Practiced

Type of Driving (City, Highway, Rural...)

Day Minutes		Night Minutes		Total Minutes	
Carried Forward		Carried Forward		Carried Forward	
Total to Date		Total to Date		Total to Date	

Notes

Instructor	
Instructor's Signature	

Date	

Time Started		Time Finished	

Weather Conditions	

Skills Practiced

Type of Driving (City, Highway, Rural...)

Day Minutes		Night Minutes		Total Minutes	
Carried Forward		Carried Forward		Carried Forward	
Total to Date		Total to Date		Total to Date	

Notes

Instructor	
Instructor's Signature	

Date	

Time Started		Time Finished	

Weather Conditions	

Skills Practiced

Type of Driving (City, Highway, Rural…)

Day Minutes		Night Minutes		Total Minutes	
Carried Forward		Carried Forward		Carried Forward	
Total to Date		Total to Date		Total to Date	

Notes

Instructor	

Instructor's Signature	

Date	

Time Started		Time Finished	

Weather Conditions	

Skills Practiced

Type of Driving (City, Highway, Rural…)

Day Minutes		Night Minutes		Total Minutes	
Carried Forward		Carried Forward		Carried Forward	
Total to Date		Total to Date		Total to Date	

Notes

Instructor	

Instructor's Signature	

Date	

Time Started		Time Finished	

Weather Conditions	

Skills Practiced

Type of Driving (City, Highway, Rural...)

Day Minutes		Night Minutes		Total Minutes	
Carried Forward		Carried Forward		Carried Forward	
Total to Date		Total to Date		Total to Date	

Notes

Instructor	

Instructor's Signature	

Date	

Time Started		Time Finished	

Weather Conditions	

Skills Practiced

Type of Driving (City, Highway, Rural...)

Day Minutes		Night Minutes		Total Minutes	
Carried Forward		Carried Forward		Carried Forward	
Total to Date		Total to Date		Total to Date	

Notes

Instructor	

Instructor's Signature	

Date	

Time Started		Time Finished	

Weather Conditions	

Skills Practiced

Type of Driving (City, Highway, Rural…)

Day Minutes		Night Minutes		Total Minutes	
Carried Forward		Carried Forward		Carried Forward	
Total to Date		Total to Date		Total to Date	

Notes

Instructor	

Instructor's Signature	

Date	

Time Started		Time Finished	

Weather Conditions	

Skills Practiced

Type of Driving (City, Highway, Rural…)

Day Minutes		Night Minutes		Total Minutes	
Carried Forward		Carried Forward		Carried Forward	
Total to Date		Total to Date		Total to Date	

Notes

Instructor	

Instructor's Signature	

Date	

Time Started		Time Finished	

Weather Conditions	

Skills Practiced

Type of Driving (City, Highway, Rural...)

Day Minutes		Night Minutes		Total Minutes	
Carried Forward		Carried Forward		Carried Forward	
Total to Date		Total to Date		Total to Date	

Notes

Instructor	
Instructor's Signature	

Date	

Time Started		Time Finished	

Weather Conditions	

Skills Practiced

Type of Driving (City, Highway, Rural...)

Day Minutes		Night Minutes		Total Minutes	
Carried Forward		Carried Forward		Carried Forward	
Total to Date		Total to Date		Total to Date	

Notes

Instructor	
Instructor's Signature	

Date	

Time Started		Time Finished	

Weather Conditions	

Skills Practiced

Type of Driving (City, Highway, Rural...)

Day Minutes		Night Minutes		Total Minutes	
Carried Forward		Carried Forward		Carried Forward	
Total to Date		Total to Date		Total to Date	

Notes

Instructor	

Instructor's Signature	

Date	

Time Started		Time Finished	

Weather Conditions	

Skills Practiced

Type of Driving (City, Highway, Rural...)

Day Minutes		Night Minutes		Total Minutes	
Carried Forward		Carried Forward		Carried Forward	
Total to Date		Total to Date		Total to Date	

Notes

Instructor	

Instructor's Signature	

Date	

Time Started		Time Finished	

Weather Conditions	

Skills Practiced

Type of Driving (City, Highway, Rural...)

Day Minutes		Night Minutes		Total Minutes	
Carried Forward		Carried Forward		Carried Forward	
Total to Date		Total to Date		Total to Date	

Notes

Instructor	
Instructor's Signature	

Date	

Time Started		Time Finished	

Weather Conditions	

Skills Practiced

Type of Driving (City, Highway, Rural...)

Day Minutes		Night Minutes		Total Minutes	
Carried Forward		Carried Forward		Carried Forward	
Total to Date		Total to Date		Total to Date	

Notes

Instructor	
Instructor's Signature	

Date	

Time Started		Time Finished	

Weather Conditions	

Skills Practiced

Type of Driving (City, Highway, Rural...)

Day Minutes		Night Minutes		Total Minutes	
Carried Forward		Carried Forward		Carried Forward	
Total to Date		Total to Date		Total to Date	

Notes

Instructor	

Instructor's Signature	

Date	

Time Started		Time Finished	

Weather Conditions	

Skills Practiced

Type of Driving (City, Highway, Rural...)

Day Minutes		Night Minutes		Total Minutes	
Carried Forward		Carried Forward		Carried Forward	
Total to Date		Total to Date		Total to Date	

Notes

Instructor	

Instructor's Signature	

Date	

Time Started		Time Finished	

Weather Conditions	

Skills Practiced

Type of Driving (City, Highway, Rural...)

Day Minutes		Night Minutes		Total Minutes	
Carried Forward		Carried Forward		Carried Forward	
Total to Date		Total to Date		Total to Date	

Notes

Instructor	

Instructor's Signature	

Date	

Time Started		Time Finished	

Weather Conditions	

Skills Practiced

Type of Driving (City, Highway, Rural...)

Day Minutes		Night Minutes		Total Minutes	
Carried Forward		Carried Forward		Carried Forward	
Total to Date		Total to Date		Total to Date	

Notes

Instructor	

Instructor's Signature	

Date	

Time Started		Time Finished	

Weather Conditions	

Skills Practiced

Type of Driving (City, Highway, Rural...)

Day Minutes		Night Minutes		Total Minutes	
Carried Forward		Carried Forward		Carried Forward	
Total to Date		Total to Date		Total to Date	

Notes

Instructor	

Instructor's Signature	

Date	

Time Started		Time Finished	

Weather Conditions	

Skills Practiced

Type of Driving (City, Highway, Rural...)

Day Minutes		Night Minutes		Total Minutes	
Carried Forward		Carried Forward		Carried Forward	
Total to Date		Total to Date		Total to Date	

Notes

Instructor	

Instructor's Signature	

Date	

Time Started		Time Finished	

Weather Conditions	

Skills Practiced

Type of Driving (City, Highway, Rural...)

Day Minutes		Night Minutes		Total Minutes	
Carried Forward		Carried Forward		Carried Forward	
Total to Date		Total to Date		Total to Date	

Notes

Instructor	

Instructor's Signature	

Date	

Time Started		Time Finished	

Weather Conditions	

Skills Practiced

Type of Driving (City, Highway, Rural...)

Day Minutes		Night Minutes		Total Minutes	
Carried Forward		Carried Forward		Carried Forward	
Total to Date		Total to Date		Total to Date	

Notes

Instructor	

Instructor's Signature	

Date	

Time Started		Time Finished	

Weather Conditions

Skills Practiced

Type of Driving (City, Highway, Rural...)

Day Minutes		Night Minutes		Total Minutes	
Carried Forward		Carried Forward		Carried Forward	
Total to Date		Total to Date		Total to Date	

Notes

Instructor	

Instructor's Signature	

Date	

Time Started		Time Finished	

Weather Conditions

Skills Practiced

Type of Driving (City, Highway, Rural...)

Day Minutes		Night Minutes		Total Minutes	
Carried Forward		Carried Forward		Carried Forward	
Total to Date		Total to Date		Total to Date	

Notes

Instructor	

Instructor's Signature	

Date	
Time Started		**Time Finished**	
Weather Conditions	
Skills Practiced	
Type of Driving (City, Highway, Rural...)	

Day Minutes		Night Minutes		Total Minutes	
Carried Forward		Carried Forward		Carried Forward	
Total to Date		Total to Date		Total to Date	

Notes

Instructor	
Instructor's Signature	

Date	
Time Started		**Time Finished**	
Weather Conditions	
Skills Practiced	
Type of Driving (City, Highway, Rural...)	

Day Minutes		Night Minutes		Total Minutes	
Carried Forward		Carried Forward		Carried Forward	
Total to Date		Total to Date		Total to Date	

Notes

Instructor	
Instructor's Signature	

Date	
Time Started			Time Finished	
Weather Conditions	
Skills Practiced	
Type of Driving (City, Highway, Rural...)	

Day Minutes		Night Minutes		Total Minutes	
Carried Forward		Carried Forward		Carried Forward	
Total to Date		Total to Date		Total to Date	

Notes	
Instructor	
Instructor's Signature	

Date	
Time Started			Time Finished	
Weather Conditions	
Skills Practiced	
Type of Driving (City, Highway, Rural...)	

Day Minutes		Night Minutes		Total Minutes	
Carried Forward		Carried Forward		Carried Forward	
Total to Date		Total to Date		Total to Date	

Notes	
Instructor	
Instructor's Signature	

Date	

Time Started		Time Finished	

Weather Conditions	

Skills Practiced

Type of Driving (City, Highway, Rural...)

Day Minutes		Night Minutes		Total Minutes	
Carried Forward		Carried Forward		Carried Forward	
Total to Date		Total to Date		Total to Date	

Notes

Instructor	

Instructor's Signature	

Date	

Time Started		Time Finished	

Weather Conditions	

Skills Practiced

Type of Driving (City, Highway, Rural...)

Day Minutes		Night Minutes		Total Minutes	
Carried Forward		Carried Forward		Carried Forward	
Total to Date		Total to Date		Total to Date	

Notes

Instructor	

Instructor's Signature	

Date	

Time Started		Time Finished	

Weather Conditions	

Skills Practiced

Type of Driving (City, Highway, Rural...)

Day Minutes		Night Minutes		Total Minutes	
Carried Forward		Carried Forward		Carried Forward	
Total to Date		Total to Date		Total to Date	

Notes

Instructor	

Instructor's Signature	

Date	

Time Started		Time Finished	

Weather Conditions	

Skills Practiced

Type of Driving (City, Highway, Rural...)

Day Minutes		Night Minutes		Total Minutes	
Carried Forward		Carried Forward		Carried Forward	
Total to Date		Total to Date		Total to Date	

Notes

Instructor	

Instructor's Signature	

Date	

Time Started		Time Finished	

Weather Conditions	

Skills Practiced

Type of Driving (City, Highway, Rural...)

Day Minutes		Night Minutes		Total Minutes	
Carried Forward		Carried Forward		Carried Forward	
Total to Date		Total to Date		Total to Date	

Notes

Instructor	
Instructor's Signature	

Date	

Time Started		Time Finished	

Weather Conditions	

Skills Practiced

Type of Driving (City, Highway, Rural...)

Day Minutes		Night Minutes		Total Minutes	
Carried Forward		Carried Forward		Carried Forward	
Total to Date		Total to Date		Total to Date	

Notes

Instructor	
Instructor's Signature	

Date	

Time Started		Time Finished	

Weather Conditions	

Skills Practiced

Type of Driving (City, Highway, Rural...)

Day Minutes		Night Minutes		Total Minutes	
Carried Forward		Carried Forward		Carried Forward	
Total to Date		Total to Date		Total to Date	

Notes

Instructor	
Instructor's Signature	

Date	

Time Started		Time Finished	

Weather Conditions	

Skills Practiced

Type of Driving (City, Highway, Rural...)

Day Minutes		Night Minutes		Total Minutes	
Carried Forward		Carried Forward		Carried Forward	
Total to Date		Total to Date		Total to Date	

Notes

Instructor	
Instructor's Signature	

Date	

Time Started		Time Finished	

Weather Conditions	

Skills Practiced

Type of Driving (City, Highway, Rural...)

Day Minutes		Night Minutes		Total Minutes	
Carried Forward		Carried Forward		Carried Forward	
Total to Date		Total to Date		Total to Date	

Notes

Instructor	

Instructor's Signature	

Date	

Time Started		Time Finished	

Weather Conditions	

Skills Practiced

Type of Driving (City, Highway, Rural...)

Day Minutes		Night Minutes		Total Minutes	
Carried Forward		Carried Forward		Carried Forward	
Total to Date		Total to Date		Total to Date	

Notes

Instructor	

Instructor's Signature	

Date	

Time Started		Time Finished	

Weather Conditions	

Skills Practiced

Type of Driving (City, Highway, Rural...)

Day Minutes		Night Minutes		Total Minutes	
Carried Forward		Carried Forward		Carried Forward	
Total to Date		Total to Date		Total to Date	

Notes

Instructor	
Instructor's Signature	

Date	

Time Started		Time Finished	

Weather Conditions	

Skills Practiced

Type of Driving (City, Highway, Rural...)

Day Minutes		Night Minutes		Total Minutes	
Carried Forward		Carried Forward		Carried Forward	
Total to Date		Total to Date		Total to Date	

Notes

Instructor	
Instructor's Signature	

Date	

Time Started		Time Finished	

Weather Conditions	

Skills Practiced

Type of Driving (City, Highway, Rural...)

Day Minutes		Night Minutes		Total Minutes	
Carried Forward		Carried Forward		Carried Forward	
Total to Date		Total to Date		Total to Date	

Notes

Instructor	

Instructor's Signature	

Date	

Time Started		Time Finished	

Weather Conditions	

Skills Practiced

Type of Driving (City, Highway, Rural...)

Day Minutes		Night Minutes		Total Minutes	
Carried Forward		Carried Forward		Carried Forward	
Total to Date		Total to Date		Total to Date	

Notes

Instructor	

Instructor's Signature	

Date	

Time Started		Time Finished	

Weather Conditions	

Skills Practiced

Type of Driving (City, Highway, Rural...)

Day Minutes		Night Minutes		Total Minutes	
Carried Forward		Carried Forward		Carried Forward	
Total to Date		Total to Date		Total to Date	

Notes

Instructor	

Instructor's Signature	

Date	

Time Started		Time Finished	

Weather Conditions	

Skills Practiced

Type of Driving (City, Highway, Rural...)

Day Minutes		Night Minutes		Total Minutes	
Carried Forward		Carried Forward		Carried Forward	
Total to Date		Total to Date		Total to Date	

Notes

Instructor	

Instructor's Signature	

Date	

Time Started		Time Finished	

Weather Conditions	

Skills Practiced

Type of Driving (City, Highway, Rural...)

Day Minutes		Night Minutes		Total Minutes	
Carried Forward		Carried Forward		Carried Forward	
Total to Date		Total to Date		Total to Date	

Notes

Instructor	

Instructor's Signature	

Date	

Time Started		Time Finished	

Weather Conditions	

Skills Practiced

Type of Driving (City, Highway, Rural...)

Day Minutes		Night Minutes		Total Minutes	
Carried Forward		Carried Forward		Carried Forward	
Total to Date		Total to Date		Total to Date	

Notes

Instructor	

Instructor's Signature	

Date	

Time Started		Time Finished	

Weather Conditions	

Skills Practiced

Type of Driving (City, Highway, Rural...)

Day Minutes		Night Minutes		Total Minutes	
Carried Forward		Carried Forward		Carried Forward	
Total to Date		Total to Date		Total to Date	

Notes

Instructor	
Instructor's Signature	

Date	

Time Started		Time Finished	

Weather Conditions	

Skills Practiced

Type of Driving (City, Highway, Rural...)

Day Minutes		Night Minutes		Total Minutes	
Carried Forward		Carried Forward		Carried Forward	
Total to Date		Total to Date		Total to Date	

Notes

Instructor	
Instructor's Signature	

Date	

Time Started			Time Finished	

Weather Conditions	

Skills Practiced	

Type of Driving (City, Highway, Rural...)	

Day Minutes		Night Minutes		Total Minutes	
Carried Forward		Carried Forward		Carried Forward	
Total to Date		Total to Date		Total to Date	

Notes	

Instructor	

Instructor's Signature	

Date	

Time Started			Time Finished	

Weather Conditions	

Skills Practiced	

Type of Driving (City, Highway, Rural...)	

Day Minutes		Night Minutes		Total Minutes	
Carried Forward		Carried Forward		Carried Forward	
Total to Date		Total to Date		Total to Date	

Notes	

Instructor	

Instructor's Signature	

Date	

Time Started		Time Finished	

Weather Conditions	

Skills Practiced

Type of Driving (City, Highway, Rural...)

Day Minutes		Night Minutes		Total Minutes	
Carried Forward		Carried Forward		Carried Forward	
Total to Date		Total to Date		Total to Date	

Notes

Instructor	
Instructor's Signature	

Date	

Time Started		Time Finished	

Weather Conditions	

Skills Practiced

Type of Driving (City, Highway, Rural...)

Day Minutes		Night Minutes		Total Minutes	
Carried Forward		Carried Forward		Carried Forward	
Total to Date		Total to Date		Total to Date	

Notes

Instructor	
Instructor's Signature	

Date	

Time Started		Time Finished	

Weather Conditions	

Skills Practiced

Type of Driving (City, Highway, Rural...)

Day Minutes		Night Minutes		Total Minutes	
Carried Forward		Carried Forward		Carried Forward	
Total to Date		Total to Date		Total to Date	

Notes

Instructor	

Instructor's Signature	

Date	

Time Started		Time Finished	

Weather Conditions	

Skills Practiced

Type of Driving (City, Highway, Rural...)

Day Minutes		Night Minutes		Total Minutes	
Carried Forward		Carried Forward		Carried Forward	
Total to Date		Total to Date		Total to Date	

Notes

Instructor	

Instructor's Signature	

Date	

Time Started		Time Finished	

Weather Conditions	

Skills Practiced

Type of Driving (City, Highway, Rural...)

Day Minutes		Night Minutes		Total Minutes	
Carried Forward		Carried Forward		Carried Forward	
Total to Date		Total to Date		Total to Date	

Notes

Instructor	
Instructor's Signature	

Date	

Time Started		Time Finished	

Weather Conditions	

Skills Practiced

Type of Driving (City, Highway, Rural...)

Day Minutes		Night Minutes		Total Minutes	
Carried Forward		Carried Forward		Carried Forward	
Total to Date		Total to Date		Total to Date	

Notes

Instructor	
Instructor's Signature	

Date	

Time Started		Time Finished	

Weather Conditions	

Skills Practiced

Type of Driving (City, Highway, Rural...)

Day Minutes		Night Minutes		Total Minutes	
Carried Forward		Carried Forward		Carried Forward	
Total to Date		Total to Date		Total to Date	

Notes

Instructor	

Instructor's Signature	

Date	

Time Started		Time Finished	

Weather Conditions	

Skills Practiced

Type of Driving (City, Highway, Rural...)

Day Minutes		Night Minutes		Total Minutes	
Carried Forward		Carried Forward		Carried Forward	
Total to Date		Total to Date		Total to Date	

Notes

Instructor	

Instructor's Signature	

Date	

Time Started		Time Finished	

Weather Conditions	

Skills Practiced

Type of Driving (City, Highway, Rural...)

Day Minutes		Night Minutes		Total Minutes	
Carried Forward		Carried Forward		Carried Forward	
Total to Date		Total to Date		Total to Date	

Notes

Instructor	

Instructor's Signature	

Date	

Time Started		Time Finished	

Weather Conditions	

Skills Practiced

Type of Driving (City, Highway, Rural...)

Day Minutes		Night Minutes		Total Minutes	
Carried Forward		Carried Forward		Carried Forward	
Total to Date		Total to Date		Total to Date	

Notes

Instructor	

Instructor's Signature	

Date	
Time Started		Time Finished	
Weather Conditions	
Skills Practiced	

| Type of Driving (City, Highway, Rural...) |

Day Minutes		Night Minutes		Total Minutes	
Carried Forward		Carried Forward		Carried Forward	
Total to Date		Total to Date		Total to Date	

Notes	
Instructor	
Instructor's Signature	

Date	
Time Started		Time Finished	
Weather Conditions	
Skills Practiced	

| Type of Driving (City, Highway, Rural...) |

Day Minutes		Night Minutes		Total Minutes	
Carried Forward		Carried Forward		Carried Forward	
Total to Date		Total to Date		Total to Date	

Notes	
Instructor	
Instructor's Signature	

Date	

Time Started		Time Finished	

Weather Conditions	

Skills Practiced

Type of Driving (City, Highway, Rural...)

Day Minutes		Night Minutes		Total Minutes	
Carried Forward		Carried Forward		Carried Forward	
Total to Date		Total to Date		Total to Date	

Notes

Instructor	

Instructor's Signature	

Date	

Time Started		Time Finished	

Weather Conditions	

Skills Practiced

Type of Driving (City, Highway, Rural...)

Day Minutes		Night Minutes		Total Minutes	
Carried Forward		Carried Forward		Carried Forward	
Total to Date		Total to Date		Total to Date	

Notes

Instructor	

Instructor's Signature	

Date	

Time Started		Time Finished	

Weather Conditions	

Skills Practiced

Type of Driving (City, Highway, Rural...)

Day Minutes		Night Minutes		Total Minutes	
Carried Forward		Carried Forward		Carried Forward	
Total to Date		Total to Date		Total to Date	

Notes

Instructor	
Instructor's Signature	

Date	

Time Started		Time Finished	

Weather Conditions	

Skills Practiced

Type of Driving (City, Highway, Rural...)

Day Minutes		Night Minutes		Total Minutes	
Carried Forward		Carried Forward		Carried Forward	
Total to Date		Total to Date		Total to Date	

Notes

Instructor	
Instructor's Signature	

Date	

Time Started		Time Finished	

Weather Conditions	

Skills Practiced

Type of Driving (City, Highway, Rural...)

Day Minutes		Night Minutes		Total Minutes	
Carried Forward		Carried Forward		Carried Forward	
Total to Date		Total to Date		Total to Date	

Notes

Instructor	

Instructor's Signature	

Date	

Time Started		Time Finished	

Weather Conditions	

Skills Practiced

Type of Driving (City, Highway, Rural...)

Day Minutes		Night Minutes		Total Minutes	
Carried Forward		Carried Forward		Carried Forward	
Total to Date		Total to Date		Total to Date	

Notes

Instructor	

Instructor's Signature	

Date	

Time Started		Time Finished	

Weather Conditions	

Skills Practiced

Type of Driving (City, Highway, Rural...)

Day Minutes		Night Minutes		Total Minutes	
Carried Forward		Carried Forward		Carried Forward	
Total to Date		Total to Date		Total to Date	

Notes

Instructor	
Instructor's Signature	

Date	

Time Started		Time Finished	

Weather Conditions	

Skills Practiced

Type of Driving (City, Highway, Rural...)

Day Minutes		Night Minutes		Total Minutes	
Carried Forward		Carried Forward		Carried Forward	
Total to Date		Total to Date		Total to Date	

Notes

Instructor	
Instructor's Signature	

Date	

Time Started		Time Finished	

Weather Conditions	

Skills Practiced

Type of Driving (City, Highway, Rural...)

Day Minutes		Night Minutes		Total Minutes	
Carried Forward		Carried Forward		Carried Forward	
Total to Date		Total to Date		Total to Date	

Notes

Instructor	

Instructor's Signature	

Date	

Time Started		Time Finished	

Weather Conditions	

Skills Practiced

Type of Driving (City, Highway, Rural...)

Day Minutes		Night Minutes		Total Minutes	
Carried Forward		Carried Forward		Carried Forward	
Total to Date		Total to Date		Total to Date	

Notes

Instructor	

Instructor's Signature	

Date	

Time Started		Time Finished	

Weather Conditions	

Skills Practiced

Type of Driving (City, Highway, Rural...)

Day Minutes		Night Minutes		Total Minutes	
Carried Forward		Carried Forward		Carried Forward	
Total to Date		Total to Date		Total to Date	

Notes

Instructor	

Instructor's Signature	

Date	

Time Started		Time Finished	

Weather Conditions	

Skills Practiced

Type of Driving (City, Highway, Rural...)

Day Minutes		Night Minutes		Total Minutes	
Carried Forward		Carried Forward		Carried Forward	
Total to Date		Total to Date		Total to Date	

Notes

Instructor	

Instructor's Signature	

Date	
Time Started		Time Finished	
Weather Conditions	
Skills Practiced	
Type of Driving (City, Highway, Rural...)	

Day Minutes		Night Minutes		Total Minutes	
Carried Forward		Carried Forward		Carried Forward	
Total to Date		Total to Date		Total to Date	

Notes	
Instructor	
Instructor's Signature	

Date	
Time Started		Time Finished	
Weather Conditions	
Skills Practiced	
Type of Driving (City, Highway, Rural...)	

Day Minutes		Night Minutes		Total Minutes	
Carried Forward		Carried Forward		Carried Forward	
Total to Date		Total to Date		Total to Date	

Notes	
Instructor	
Instructor's Signature	

Date	

Time Started		Time Finished	

Weather Conditions	

Skills Practiced

Type of Driving (City, Highway, Rural...)

Day Minutes		Night Minutes		Total Minutes	
Carried Forward		Carried Forward		Carried Forward	
Total to Date		Total to Date		Total to Date	

Notes

Instructor	

Instructor's Signature	

Date	

Time Started		Time Finished	

Weather Conditions	

Skills Practiced

Type of Driving (City, Highway, Rural...)

Day Minutes		Night Minutes		Total Minutes	
Carried Forward		Carried Forward		Carried Forward	
Total to Date		Total to Date		Total to Date	

Notes

Instructor	

Instructor's Signature	

THANK YOU FOR CHOOSING

DENBARNES PRESS

WE HOPE YOU ENJOYED THIS BOOK!

Did it help you in staying organized?

Any suggestions or ideas on how to improve it?

LET US KNOW

BY WRITING US A REVIEW!